Brett fires a pass against Dallas.

ELECTRIC FOOTBALL GAME

Quarterback Brett Favre dropped back to pass. Dallas Cowboys **defenders** rushed at him. He saw **wide receiver** Sidney Rice sprinting down the field. Brett stepped up and threw high and far. The football sailed through the air and

TABLE OF CONTENTS

Lerner Publications Company
A division of Lerner Publishing Group, Inc.
241 First Avenue North
Minneapolis, MN 55401 U.S.A.

Website address: www.lernerbooks.com

Library of Congress Cataloging-in-Publication Data

Savage, Jeff.
    Brett Favre / by Jeff Savage.
      p.   cm. — (Amazing athletes)
    Includes bibliographical references and index.
    ISBN 978-0-7613-6651-5 (lib. bdg. : alk. paper)
    1. Favre, Brett—Juvenile literature. 2. Football players—United States—Biography—Juvenile literature. 3. Quarterbacks (Football)—United States—Biography—Juvenile literature. I. Title.
GV939.F29S276 2011
796.332092—dc22 [B]   2010009346

Manufactured in the United States of America
1 — BP — 7/15/10

Brett Favre

By Jeff Savage

AMAZING ATHLETES

Lerner Publications Company • Minneapolis

dropped into Rice's hands. **Touchdown**! Brett and the Minnesota Vikings had scored first on a 47-yard bomb!

Over 63,000 fans filled Mall of America Field in Minnesota for this 2010 National Football League (NFL) **playoff** game. Thousands of people were wearing purple or white number 4 jerseys in support of Brett. They were hoping the **veteran** quarterback could lead the Vikings to victory and a chance to go to the Super Bowl.

Fans at Mall of America Field cheer on Brett and the Vikings.

Brett looks down the field and gets ready to throw.

The Cowboys kicked a **field goal** to make the score 7–3. Brett went back to work. He led Minnesota down the field. Brett fired a pass to Rice for the touchdown. The Vikings led 14–3.

Minnesota had an 8–0 record at home in the regular season. Brett had thrown 21 touchdown passes with just two **interceptions** on his home field. Favre's great play was no surprise to the Vikings. The team had talked the

40-year-old out of retirement to join Minnesota just before the season began.

Two field goals by the Vikings stretched the score to 20–3. Midway through the fourth quarter, Brett struck again. He passed to Rice for a third touchdown, this time from 45 yards out. Brett raced to the **end zone** pumping his fist to celebrate. He jumped onto the back of teammate Anthony Herrera. He lifted Rice into the air. Brett was about to become the first quarterback in NFL history to win a playoff game at the age of 40.

Brett lifts Sidney Rice into the air after yet another touchdown.

Brett wasn't finished yet. With two minutes left, he threw an 11-yard touchdown to Visanthe Shiancoe. This was the first time in Brett's 19-year career that he passed for four touchdowns in a playoff game. The Vikings won, 34–3.

"That was electric," Brett said afterward. "It was really special. I enjoyed every minute. This is what I came back for."

Brett talks about the game after the Vikings' big win.

Brett grew up near Gulfport, Mississippi.

A NATURAL

Brett Lorenzo Favre was born October 10, 1969, in Gulfport, Mississippi. He grew up in the nearby town of Kiln. His father, Irvin, was a high school football coach. His mother, Bonita, was a special education teacher. Brett's two brothers, Scott and Jeff, played quarterback at Hancock High School. Brett's sister, Brandi, was Miss Teen Mississippi.

Brett was a stubborn boy. He would not drink from anyone else's cup or eat from another's plate. He slept on top of his sheets so he would not have to make his bed.

Brett got his first football uniform at the age of one. Within a few years, he was the water boy for his dad's football team. "I thought the guys on the high school team were a big deal—and they were," Brett said. "I just wanted to stand next to the starting quarterback and have folks say, 'Look, Brett actually knows that guy.'" By fourth grade, Brett could throw a football nearly as far as the high school quarterback. That year, he won a local Punt, Pass & Kick contest.

In 1983, as a high school **freshman**, Brett played wide receiver—for one play. He caught a pass and got the wind knocked out of him. He asked his dad if he could try playing quarterback.

Brett *(center)* shares a meal at home with his family.

Brett threw for two touchdowns in the game and ran for two more. "He was talented," said his father, "plus, he was smart. He was a natural."

Brett met Deanna Tynes in high school. "She was a real tomboy," said Brett, "as tough as one of the guys." Together they ate lunch, did homework, and played sports. (Years later, they would marry.)

Brett told Deanna about his goal of being a **professional** quarterback. Deanna encouraged him. But Brett didn't seem to have much of a chance. His father's offense featured mostly running plays. In some games, Brett threw only five passes. Most college teams didn't notice him. Brett played **safety** on defense and also was the team's kicker. The University of Southern Mississippi was the only college to offer Brett a football **scholarship**—as a safety. Brett eagerly said yes.

Brett looked forward to playing college football.

Brett began his college career on the bench.

LARGER THAN LIFE

In 1987 Brett started practice with the Southern Miss Golden Eagles as a safety. He told the coaches he could play quarterback. They made him the seventh-stringer. Six quarterbacks were ahead of him. But not for long. Brett fired bullet passes. He stayed after practices to work on his game. Within a month, he had moved up to third string.

Brett earned a special education teaching degree from the University of Southern Mississippi.

The Golden Eagles lost their first game of the 1987 season as Brett watched from the bench. In their next game, they were trailing in the second half against Tulane University. The first two quarterbacks had struggled. Coach Jim Carmody turned to the bench and called for Brett. Brett was so nervous as he ran onto the field that he nearly threw up. He calmed down and threw two touchdown passes to lead his team to a 31–24 victory. Brett was named the team's new starter. He was still just seventeen years old.

Southern Miss finished the season with a 5–6 record. Along the way, Brett learned to be a big-time quarterback. He'd always had a strong throwing arm. In college, he developed

"touch" by making soft throws. He learned
to fool defenders with **pump fakes**. As a
sophomore, Brett guided Southern Miss to a
10–2 record and an Independence Bowl win. As
a **junior** in 1989, Brett threw the game-winning
touchdown pass with 23 seconds left to stun
powerhouse Florida State. He had 300-yard
passing games against Texas A&M and the
University of Alabama.

Brett throws a pass
against Florida State.
The Golden Eagles won
the game, 30–26.

Before the start of the next season, Brett nearly died in a car accident. He was driving home one night from a fishing trip when his car skidded out of control. It flipped three times and crashed into a pine tree. Brett was taken to the hospital in an ambulance. He suffered a broken back and damage to his brain. Brett had surgery. He was weak. In the next month, he lost 35 pounds. People wondered if Brett would ever play football again.

Brett worked hard to regain his strength. "Every day I tried to do a little more," he said. "Gradually I fought my way back." Six weeks after the accident, Brett ran onto Legion Field in Birmingham, Alabama. Southern Miss was there to take on the Alabama Crimson Tide. He told his teammates he would lead them to victory. "My uniform [didn't] fit me. My teammates were crying," Brett said after the game. "It was unbelievable." Brett repeatedly led his team on drives into the end zone. The Golden Eagles won in the final seconds. "You can call it a miracle or a legend or whatever you want to," said Alabama coach Gene Stallings. "I just know that Brett Favre was larger than life."

Alabama coach Gene Stallings was impressed with Brett's return from injury.

When Brett's **senior** year ended, he held nearly every school passing record. He was ready for the pros. The Atlanta Falcons selected him with the 33rd pick in the 1991 NFL **Draft**. Brett wondered what the Falcons expected of him. As a **rookie**, he threw just four passes. Two were incomplete. The other two were intercepted. After the season, the Falcons traded him to the Green Bay Packers for a first-round pick. Brett's future was about to change.

Brett receives a call from the Atlanta Falcons during the 1991 NFL Draft.

Green Bay Packers fans hoped Brett would make the team a winner.

SUPER BOWL STAR

In the second game of the 1992 season, the Packers were trailing the Tampa Bay Buccaneers 17–0 at halftime. Coach Mike Holmgren benched starting quarterback Don Majkowski. He put in Brett. Brett's first pass as a Packer was caught— by Brett himself! The pass was tipped in the air and came back to Brett. He was tackled for a seven-yard loss. The Packers lost the game, 31–3.

In the next game, Majkowski got injured. Brett returned to the field against the Cincinnati Bengals. He was named the starting quarterback for the rest of the season.

The Packers lost the final game of the season and missed the playoffs. But Brett showed that he belonged in the league. He was selected for the **Pro Bowl**. At 23 years old, he was the youngest quarterback ever chosen.

Brett was having fun. He played pranks on his teammates. They enjoyed his humor. Even more, they liked his leadership. Brett guided the Packers

Brett's strong arm helped him succeed in the NFL.

Brett has always liked to have fun and play around with his teammates.

to the playoffs for the 1993 season. Their first playoff game was against the Detroit Lions. The Packers trailed, 24–21, with one minute left. Brett escaped the pass rush and fired a pass 60 yards. Sterling Sharpe caught it for the win. It was Green Bay's first playoff victory in 11 years. Brett was so excited he almost fainted.

Brett had a great season in 1995. The team won two playoff games but did not reach the Super Bowl.

The Packers lost the following week to the Dallas Cowboys. But Brett had become a star. The 1994 season was nearly the same. The Packers beat the Lions in the playoffs and then lost to the Cowboys. In 1995, Brett threw 38 touchdown passes to break the National Football Conference (NFC) single-season record. He was named the league's Most Valuable Player (MVP). This time, the Packers won two playoff games. They were one win away from reaching the Super Bowl. But they lost to the Cowboys for the third year in a row.

Brett and the Packers had another great season in 1996. This time, the team made it all the way to the Super Bowl. The game was played at the Louisiana Superdome, a short drive from Brett's hometown. On his first pass, Brett threw a 54-yard touchdown to Andre Rison. Later, he threw an 81-yard pass to Antonio Freeman to set the Super Bowl record for longest touchdown pass. Brett ran 12 yards for another score. The Packers beat the New England Patriots, 35–21.

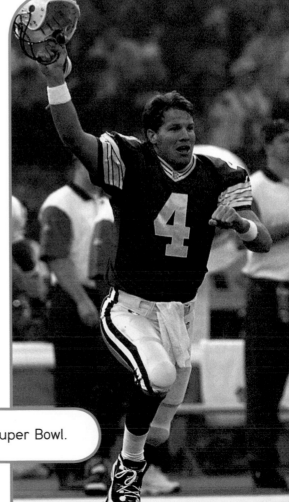

Brett celebrates on the field during the Super Bowl.

Brett has established the Brett Favre Fourward Foundation to help others. His annual golf tournament, celebrity softball game, and fund-raising dinners have raised more than $3 million for charities.

"It's the greatest feeling in the world," Brett said. "But now I'm greedy. Now I want to win more." Brett got another chance when the Packers returned to the Super Bowl after the 1997 season. But this time, they lost to the Denver Broncos, 31–24.

The Packers would not return to the Super Bowl with Brett. Green Bay reached the NFC Championship Game again in 2008. Brett's last pass as a Packer was intercepted in overtime. Green Bay lost to the New York Giants. The pass was a heartbreaking way to end a wonderful career in Green Bay. On March 4, 2008, Brett announced his retirement.

Brett joined the New York Jets in 2008.

STILL A GOOFBALL

Three months after Brett retired, he unretired.
But the Packers had moved on with a new
quarterback. Green Bay traded Brett to the New
York Jets. New Yorkers were thrilled. In two
days, they bought more than 20,000 green and
white Favre jerseys.

Brett has two daughters, Brittany (born in 1989) and Breleigh (born in 1999).

Brett led the Jets to an 8–3 record in their first 11 games. In a win over the Arizona Cardinals, he threw six touchdown passes— one less than the NFL record for a game. But Brett's shoulder began to hurt. He struggled to throw. The Jets lost four of their last five games and missed the playoffs. Afterward, the Jets revealed that Brett had a torn part of his shoulder. He told the Jets he was retiring again. The team let him go.

Brett wanted to reach the Super Bowl once more. The Minnesota Vikings took note. They had never won a Super Bowl in their 48-year history. They asked Brett for help. His shoulder was feeling better after surgery. He agreed to join the team for the 2009 season.

Brett seized control of the team right away. He led the Vikings to three straight wins to start the season. In one game, Brett threw a last-play touchdown pass to beat the San Francisco 49ers. In Week 4, the Packers came to Minnesota for *Monday Night Football*. More viewers watched this game than any other program in cable television history at the time. They saw Brett lead the Vikings to a 30–23 victory. Brett became the only player ever to beat all 32 NFL teams.

With Brett leading the way, the Vikings are a tough team to beat.

The Vikings won 10 of their first 11 games and cruised into the playoffs. They crushed the Cowboys to reach the NFC Championship Game against the New Orleans Saints. In New Orleans, Brett was battered by Saints defenders. He played with courage and nearly led his team to the Super Bowl. In the end, his final pass was intercepted to force overtime. The Saints kicked a field goal to win, 31–28.

Brett finished 2009 with his best statistical season ever. He holds nearly every quarterback record. And at 40 years old, Brett doesn't seem to be slowing down. He still plays pranks on teammates and lifts them in the air to celebrate touchdowns. "He's still a goofball," says longtime teammate Ryan Longwell.

Selected Career Highlights

2009   Set the NFL all-time record with 285 straight starts
Set NFL all-time records for completions, yards, and touchdowns
Set career high with 107.2 passer rating
Selected to Pro Bowl

2008   Selected to Pro Bowl
Threw six touchdown passes in a single game

2007   Set NFL career record with 421 touchdown passes
Named *Sports Illustrated* Sportsman of the Year
Selected to Pro Bowl

2006   Set career high with 613 passing attempts

2005   Set career highs with 372 completions and 602 passing attempts

2003   Selected to Pro Bowl

2002   Selected to Pro Bowl

2001   Selected to Pro Bowl

1997   Named NFL Most Valuable Player for the third time
Led Packers to Super Bowl
Selected to Pro Bowl

1996   Named NFL Most Valuable Player for the second time
Led Packers to Super Bowl title
Set NFC record with 39 touchdown passes
Selected to Pro Bowl

1995   Named NFL Most Valuable Player
Passed for a career high 4,413 yards
Set NFC record with 38 touchdown passes
Selected to Pro Bowl

1993   Selected to Pro Bowl

1992   Selected to Pro Bowl
Started consecutive games-played streak with Packers

1991   Drafted by Atlanta Falcons in the second round

1990	Set Southern Mississippi career records for completions, yards, and touchdowns
1989	Led Southern Mississippi to 30–26 upset of Florida State
1988	Led Southern Mississippi to 10–2 record and bowl victory
1987	Became starting quarterback for Southern Mississippi as a 17-year-old freshman

Glossary

defenders: players whose job it is to stop the other team from scoring

draft: a yearly event in which professional teams take turns choosing new players from a group

end zone: the area beyond the goal line at each end of the field. A team scores six points when it reaches the other team's end zone.

field goal: a successful kick over the crossbar and between the two upright poles. A field goal is worth three points.

freshman: first year of high school or college

interceptions: passes caught by a player on the defense. Interceptions result in the opposing team getting control of the ball.

junior: third year of high school or college

playoffs: a series of contests played after the regular season to help decide which teams will play in the Super Bowl.

Pro Bowl: a game played after the season by the top players in the NFL

professional: being paid money to play a sport

pump fakes: moves a quarterback makes by pretending to throw the ball in one direction but holding on to the ball and throwing it to another part of the field

quarterback: a player whose main job is to throw passes

rookie: a player who is playing his or her first season

safety: a defender whose main job is to stop passes to wide receivers

scholarship: money awarded to a student to help pay the cost of attending college

senior: fourth year of high school or college

sophomore: second year of high school or college

touchdown: a six-point score. A team scores a touchdown when it gets into the other team's end zone with the ball.

veteran: a player with years of experience

wide receiver: an offensive player whose main job is to catch passes

Further Reading & Websites

Kennedy, Mike, and Mark Stewart. *Touchdown: The Power and Precision of Football's Perfect Play.* Minneapolis: Millbrook Press, 2010.

Preller, James. *NFL: Super Bowl Super Quarterbacks.* New York: Scholastic, 2005.

Savage, Jeff. *Adrian Peterson.* Minneapolis: Lerner Publications Company, 2011.

Brett's Official Site
http://www.officialbrettfavre.com
Brett's official website features a biography, photos, and the latest news about Brett. Information about his fan club and how to get Brett Favre autographed helmets, footballs, signed posters, and more are also included.

Minnesota Vikings: The Official Site
http://www.vikings.com
The official website of the Minnesota Vikings includes the team schedule and game results, late-breaking news, biographies of Brett Favre and other players and coaches, and much more.

Sports Illustrated Kids
http://www.sikids.com
The *Sports Illustrated Kids* website covers all sports, including football.

Index

Photo Acknowledgments

Photographs are used with the permission of: AP Photo/Charlie Neibergal, p. 4; AP Photo/David Stluka, pp. 5, 8, 20, 22, 27, 29; AP Photo/James D. Smith, p. 6; AP Photo/Paul Sancya, p. 7; © iStockphoto.com/Kathy Hicks, p. 9; © Ronald C. Modra/Sports Illustrated/Getty Images, p. 11; Seth Poppel Yearbook Library, p. 12; © Allen Steele/Getty Images, pp. 13, 15; AP Photo/stf, p. 17; AP Photo/Sun Herald, Tim Isbell, p. 18; © Rick Stewart/Getty Images, p. 19; © Allen Eyestone/Palm Beach Post/ZUMA Press, p. 21; AP Photo/Doug Mills, p. 23; AP Photo/John Russell, p. 25

Front cover: © Larry French/Getty Images.